Lancashire's Lost Railwa

by

David James

CW00661764

A Lancashire & Yorkshire Railway 4-4-2 locomotive, No. 12, at Blackpool Central Station.

Text © David James, 2004.
First published in the United Kingdom, 2004,
reprinted 2013
by Stenlake Publishing Ltd.,
01290 551122
www.stenlake.co.uk

ISBN 9781840332889

**The publishers regret that they cannot supply
copies of any pictures featured in this book.**

PICTURE ACKNOWLEDGEMENTS
The publishers wish to thank the following for contributing photographs
to this book: John Alsop for the front cover, pages 1, 6–8, 10, 13, 14, 17, 18,
20, 21, 23, 24, 27–29, 31–37, 39–41, 43–46, 48 and the back cover; Richard
Casserley for the inside front cover and pages 2, 4, 5, 9, 11, 12, 15, 16, 19, 22,
25, 26, 30, 38, 42 and 47.

**Greenfield Station opened on 1 August 1849
and remains open for passenger services.**

INTRODUCTION

Lancashire can justifiably claim to be the birthplace of Britain's Industrial Revolution during the late eighteenth and early nineteenth centuries. One of the oldest counties in the country, it was the centre for a blossoming cotton industry which dominated the expanding city of Manchester and surrounding towns such as Oldham, Rochdale, Preston, Bury and Blackburn. Raw materials for this lucrative industry were imported via the growing port of Liverpool which also exported finished textile goods all over the world. Rich coal seams began to be mined in south Lancashire, leading to the growth of towns such as Wigan and Leigh, while over at St Helens a booming chemical and glass-making trade led to further development in that area.

Once a viable railway had been proven in north-east England (the Stockton & Darlington Railway) the leading industrialists and entrepreneurs of Lancashire began pushing for similar links across the county. Rail transport offered the possibility of moving bulk loads at speed and with much reduced costs. Not only could these products be sent to Liverpool for overseas sales, but they could also be easily moved around other parts of Britain.

The railways not only benefited the county's industries but also its expanding population. Local trains transported businessmen from their homes in the suburbs and factory workers from the inner-city districts to and from their places of work. The introduction of the concept of annual summer holidays by the seaside for the masses led to the railways spreading to Lancashire's coastline where small villages such as Blackpool and Southport grew rapidly into popular resorts.

Once the Liverpool & Manchester Railway had opened, a whole host of companies sprang up throughout Lancashire to construct new lines. Many of these early companies eventually merged together to form larger enterprises or were swallowed up by bigger, more powerful rivals. Two of the biggest players in the county were the mighty London & North Western Railway (LNWR) and its great competitor, the Lancashire & Yorkshire Railway (L&Y). Later, the Midland Railway (MR) tried to break these two firms' stranglehold on rail services by forging its own path through Lancashire.

After the 1923 Groupings these three companies all became part of the London, Midland & Scottish Railway (LMS). Although this inherited the lion's share of railways across Lancashire its chief competitor, the London North Eastern Railway (LNER), did gain a small foothold around Oldham.

Lancashire's traditional textile and coal mining industries began to suffer in the wake of the First World War, leading to mass unemployment throughout parts of the county as these old industries faded away. With their decline the railways' fortunes dipped too. Even the great port of Liverpool began to suffer as shipping firms switched to alternative, cheaper facilities.

Despite a temporary relief during the Second World War, the slow decline continued throughout the late 1940s and into the 1950s. The nationalisation of the rail system in 1948 could do little to prevent many of Lancashire's railways withering away. The advent of road haulage firms and the growth of Britain's motorway network only hastened this process, as did increasing use of the motor car by many people who had once relied on the train as their primary method of transport.

Then in 1963 came the Beeching Report which sought to salvage the rail system from total collapse by closing the majority of unprofitable branch lines. This move decimated Lancashire's already much-reduced rail network and led to the county becoming little more than a through route for a handful of major lines such as the West Coast Main Line (WCML).

The great days of railway dominance in Lancashire are now well and truly over and the cobweb of lines which once criss-crossed the county has been swept away. It is the story of these glory days and the lost lines that contributed to them that this book aims to tell. It is sometimes difficult to adhere strictly to county boundaries when writing historical accounts as most railways built in the 1800s did not conveniently start or stop at a county's borders as they existed back then. Nor do they do so today in the post-1974 redefinition of Lancashire's limits. This is especially true for several lines in south Lancashire, notably the Southport – Liverpool line built by the Southport & Cheshire Lines Extension (S&CLE). This route is very much concentrated within the present day boundaries of Merseyside and as such it is my aim to include it and other Liverpool lines in a future volume. The same rule has been applied to those lines (principally around the Oldham district) that reach out over the Pennines into neighbouring Yorkshire.

The eagle-eyed reader will also notice I have not included the famous East Lancashire Railway from Bury via Ramsbottom and Rawtenstall to Bacup. I do not consider this to be a 'lost' railway due to the fact that since 1987 large sections of the line have been opened as a commercial venture by the East Lancashire Railway Preservation Society (ELRPS) with great success. Hence it is still possible to enjoy the delights of this line and rekindle memories of such wonderfully named locations as Summerseat, Clough Fold and Stacksteads. Finally, please note that all station closure dates refer to the ending of passenger services.

Adlington – Boar's Head

Passenger service withdrawn	4 January 1960	*Stations closed*	*Date*
Distance	4 miles	White Bear (Adlington)	4 January 1960
Company	Joint Lancashire & Yorkshire/	Red Rock	26 September 1949
	Lancashire Union Railway	Boar's Head	31 January 1949

White Bear Station, looking towards Wigan, 11 April 1957.

As with the Chorley – Cherry Tree branch, the short Adlington to Boar's Head line was jointly run by the L&Y and LUR. It was constructed from the L&Y's existing Bolton – Preston line at Adlington to join with the LUR's lines around Wigan near Boar's Head. The line was heavily graded with a dominating 1 in 90 climb above Red Rock Station to contend with. A viaduct, 86 feet high, required seven iron spans to carry the line across the wide Douglas Valley, while an aqueduct was needed to cross the Lancaster Canal. The branch opened for freight in November 1869 and passenger services started the next month. Such a short, difficult line was always going to suffer but somehow the branch managed to keep running until the advent of British Railways. Eager to cut costs and faced with falling demand, British Railways shut Boar's Head and Red Rock stations during 1949 and from 1960 the whole line became a freight-only operation. This scenario didn't last long, for in May 1971 the entire line was closed down for good.

Blackpool Central – Lytham – Kirkham

Passenger service withdrawn	2 November 1964	*Stations closed*	*Date*
Distance	12.25 miles	Stony Hill **	30 September 1872
Company	Blackpool & Lytham Railway	Burlington Road ***	11 September 1939
		Gillett's Crossing ****	11 September 1939
Stations closed	*Date*	South Shore Lytham Road	14 July 1916
Blackpool Central *	2 November 1964	Wrea Green	26 June 1961

Blackpool Central Station, 26 April 1949.

* Originally known as Hound's Hill Station until 1878.
** Reopened in 1931 as Squire's Gate.
*** Closed between October 1915 and March 1920. The date given is that of the last service. The station was not officially closed until 1 January 1949.
**** Closed between October 1915 and March 1920.

A local service from Blackpool to Lytham passing Gillett's Crossing, 1924.

The coastal resorts of Blackpool and Lytham were linked together by rail in 1846 by the Preston & Wyre Railway (P&W). However, in 1861 an independent company, the Blackpool & Lytham Railway (B&L) was authorised to build a rival line between the two towns. Opened in April 1863, the B&L's Lytham Station was erected a short distance from the existing P&W one, while in Blackpool the B&L set up a terminus at Hound's Hill, roughly half a mile from the P&W's existing station on Talbot Road. In July 1871 the P&W's masters, the LNWR and L&Y, succeeded in absorbing the tiny B&L and a connecting line was added between the two Lytham stations. When this opened in 1874 the original P&W station was closed and a new link was provided through to the nearby town of Kirkham. Uncertainty as to which way railway expansion in the area would go led to both the B&L and the P&W opening or closing new stops along both lines throughout the 1870s.

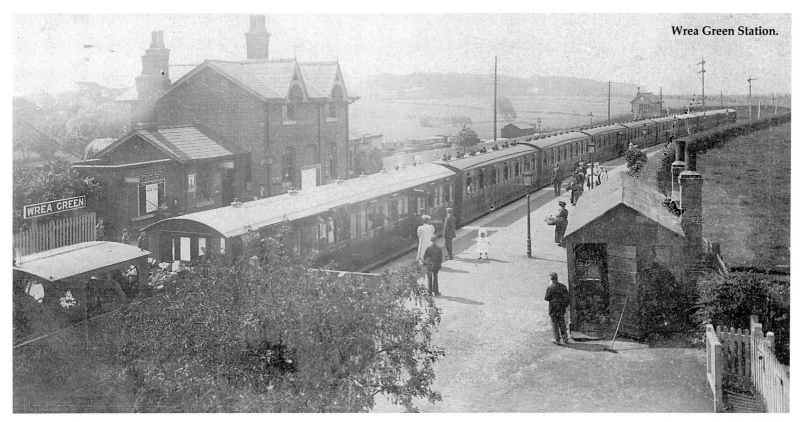

WREA GREEN

By 1900 Blackpool's population had soared to around 50,000 and the town was becoming a leading holiday resort. In order to reduce the train journey times from Kirkham to Blackpool the line into Blackpool Central (as Hound's Hill had been renamed) was shortened by 5 miles in 1903 through the opening of a direct line from Kirkham North Junction to South Shore. This stretch of track became known as the 'New Line' and soon became exceptionally busy, especially during the holiday season. In the aftermath of the First World War Blackpool was handling as many as a million holidaymakers every year. To cope with this number Central Station was provided with fourteen platforms, but even this was insufficient and congestion occurred daily as trains continuing on to Blackpool North (as Talbot Road had become) were forced to reverse back out of the station before carrying on. A plan to build a connecting line between the two stations was drafted but never implemented. After the Second World War and the abolition of petrol rationing the roads leading into Blackpool quickly filled up with motor cars and buses and the number of holidaymakers arriving at Blackpool Central dropped dramatically. In November 1964 all passenger services into Central were abandoned and trains were re-routed to terminate at Blackpool South (previously called Waterloo Road) or Blackpool North. The 'New Line' was also closed in 1965, although it continued to see infrequent use for excursion trains up until 1967.

Bolton – Bury

Passenger service withdrawn	5 October 1970	*Stations closed*	*Date*
Distance	8 miles	Bradley Fold	5 October 1970
Company	Liverpool & Bury Railway	Radcliffe Black Lane *	5 October 1970

Stations closed	*Date*
Darcy Lever	29 October 1951

* Originally known as Black Lane until 1933.

Rail services into Liverpool were originally provided by the Liverpool & Manchester Railway and its successors, the Grand Junction Railway and then the LNWR. As the city expanded, new lines to it were constructed and one of these belonged to the Liverpool & Bury Railway (L&B). The L&B's line linked the industrial towns of Bury, Bolton and Wigan to Liverpool. The stretch of line between Bury and Bolton crossed the Croal and Tonge valleys by novel high iron-lattice deck-girder viaducts supported by thickset stone pillars. It also had to reach over the

Bradley Fold Station.

Manchester, Bolton & Bury Canal and the broad River Irwell. This was achieved through the construction of two sturdy stone viaducts. When the line between the two Lancashire towns finally opened in late 1848 the L&B had joined up with the Manchester & Leeds Railway and together they formed the L&Y during 1847. To offer an alternative route between Bolton and Manchester the L&Y added a connection off the Bolton–Bury line via Radcliffe. This opened during 1879. The line between Bolton and Bury saw much heavy freight and passenger usage throughout the L&Y's lifetime and even into the days of the LMS under whose ownership the line saw the last use of ex-L&Y railmotors during 1947. A downturn in business came during the 1950s and by the 1960s the Bolton – Bury stretch was a shadow of its former self. The close proximity of the two towns meant that all too often the motor car or the bus offered a more convenient method of transport than the railway. Despite the lack of customers the line generated support in the late 1960s from many local residents strongly opposed to a plan by British Rail to scrap passenger services. Despite this opposition the scheme went ahead in October 1970. With the line closed, the trackbed between Bolton and Bury was soon lifted.

Bolton – Kenyon Junction

Passenger service withdrawn	29 March 1954		*Stations closed*	*Date*
Distance	9 miles		Chequerbent ***	3 March 1952
Company	Bolton & Leigh Railway Company		Atherton Bag Lane ****	29 March 1954
			Atherleigh	29 March 1954
Stations closed	*Date*		West Leigh *****	29 March 1954
Bolton Great Moor Street *	29 March 1954		Pennington †	29 March 1954
Rumworth & Daubhill **	3 March 1952		Kenyon Junction ††	2 January 1961

A 2-6-2T Class 2P locomotive, No. 41215, at Bolton Great Moor Street Station with the 5.05 p.m. service to Kenyon Junction, 24 April 1951.

* This replaced the first station of that name which was open between October 1849 and 1 April 1875.
** Originally known as Daubhill until 1885.
*** This replaced the first station of that name which was open between 11 June 1831 and 2 February 1885.
**** Originally known as Bag Lane until 1924.

***** Originally known as Leigh until 1876.
† Originally known as Bradshaw Leach until 1877.
†† Originally known as Bolton Junction until 1843. This station remained open to passenger services after 1954 due to its position along the former Liverpool & Manchester's Liverpool – Manchester line.

Pennington Station, 1918.

The expansion of Bolton led to a local surge in demand for coal and the easiest way of satisfying this was to increase supplies from the mines around Leigh, 7 miles to the south-west. In 1824 a local group of industrialists resolved to improve the communications between the two towns by building a rail link from Bolton to meet up with the Leeds & Liverpool Canal at Leigh. The famous George Stephenson was appointed as Chief Engineer and in 1825 Parliament gave the scheme its approval. Initially single-tracked, the line was built from Lecturers Close in Bolton up an incline at Daubhill to the collieries around Chequerbent before passing on through the mill town of Atherton and down towards Leigh and Pennington. To aid trains up the steep gradients involved, stationary steam engines were installed at Daubhill and Chequerbent. Freight trains began in August 1828, making the Bolton & Leigh (B&L) the first public railway in Lancashire to open. As the rival Liverpool & Manchester's line lay not too far to the south of Leigh, the B&L opted to connect with it by means of a short extension. This opened in January 1831 as the Kenyon & Leigh Junction Railway (K&LJ) and six months later the first passenger trains were run between Bolton and Kenyon Junction where the K&LJ joined the L&M.

Kenyon Junction Station, 23 August 1952.

Unusually, from 1836 until 1845 the line was operated privately on a contractual basis by one John Hargreaves Jnr. Hargreaves was highly successful but in 1845 the line passed to the Grand Junction Railway (GJR) after it absorbed both the B&L and the K&LJ. In turn the GJR became part of the LNWR. By this time the rival Manchester & Bolton Railway had been operating a competitive service for eight years and had pinched much of the line's potential traffic. In 1858 Great Moor Street Station was badly damaged when a runaway freight train derailed there, but the facility was patched up and soldiered on until 1874 when the LNWR built a new station of the same name. The line was also modified with double-tracks and less fearsome inclines from Bolton as far as Pennington, although it was not until 1885 that this improvement was fully completed. Although the line did well in providing connections locally, passengers wanting to travel to Liverpool were in fact better served by rival companies and many complained about their trains being delayed due to the sheer effort involved in traversing the line's gradients. Even with the support of banking engines many trains stalled during the climbs and had to set back to try again, thus prolonging journey times. With the decline of local passenger traffic after the Second World War the branch struggled to survive. In March 1954 all passenger trains were finally withdrawn due to a lack of demand. Goods services continued in diminishing numbers until the last coal train from Chequerbent ran to Bolton in October 1967.

Bury – Holcombe Brook

Passenger service withdrawn	5 May 1952	*Stations closed*	*Date*
Distance	3 miles	Holcombe Brook	5 May 1952
Company	Bury & Tottington District Railway	Tottington	5 May 1952
		Greenmount	5 May 1952
		Woolfold	5 May 1952

A 2-4-2T Class 2P locomotive, No. 50829, and coaches Nos. 3461 and 24453, with the 2.36 p.m. service from Bury at Holcombe Brook Station, 24 April 1951. This was a temporary steam service brought in after the electric service had failed.

Tottington Station.

The single-line Bury to Holcombe Brook branch was built by the Bury & Tottington District Railway Company and opened for business in 1882 with the L&Y providing the trains. Shuttle services between Bury, Tottington and Holcombe Brook accounted for most of the line's early income, although competition was fierce from the outset thanks to the development in 1883 of a local steam tram service. In 1888 the L&Y vested the line and from 1905 began introducing railmotors to work the route and save costs. However, services really improved in 1913 when Dick, Kerr & Co. of Preston used the line to experiment with high-voltage DC electric traction, employing 3,600-volt overhead power lines. This trial programme ran until 1916 when the entire branch was handed back to the L&Y which had decided for itself to electrify the route. This time a 1,200-volt DC third-rail power supply system was chosen as an extension to the earlier Manchester – Bury electrification scheme. A regular shuttle service, usually consisting of 2-car EMUs, ran from Bury to Holcombe Brook well into the days of the nationalised British Railways. However, by 1951 much of the line's electrical equipment was worn out and the cost of renewing it was unjustified for such a short stretch of track. Consequently, the popular EMUs were withdrawn in favour of ex-L&Y 2-4-2 tank engines hauling single railmotor coaches. This new working arrangement lasted until May 1952 when all passenger services along the branch ceased. Goods traffic carried on up to Tottington until August 1963 when what remained of the line was finally closed down.

Chorley – Cherry Tree

Passenger service withdrawn	4 January 1960	*Stations closed*	*Date*
Distance	8.5 miles	Heapey	4 January 1960
Company	Joint Lancashire & Yorkshire/	Brinscall	4 January 1960
	Lancashire Union Railway	Withnell	4 January 1960
		Feniscowles	4 January 1960

Brinscall Station, *c.* **1910.**

Feniscowles Station, 11 April 1957.

The Lancashire Union Railway (LUR) was keen to build links from the coalfields of south Lancashire to the textile centres in the east of the county. In 1863 the company planned to build a new line from Cherry Tree, near Blackburn, to Chorley and then on to Wigan. The L&Y, fearing a spread of the rival LNWR's influence through the LUR (rightly so, for the LUR later became part of the LNWR), objected to the idea and it was only after prolonged parliamentary debate that the scheme was approved providing it was built as a joint venture between the L&Y and LUR. The branch opened for goods trains in late 1869 and passenger services were running a month later. Building it had involved constructing two high embankments and a nine-span stone viaduct over the Lancaster Canal at Botany Brow near Chorley. Heavy gradients were a constant feature of the line, with a particularly demanding 1 in 60 climb at Brinscall. The line survived the worst ravages of the Great Depression due to the fact that the area around Chorley was less dependent on the textile trade than others and had successful bleaching and printing industries to keep it going. There was also a small coal-mining sector and quarrying business nearby which contributed to the branch's freight flows and in the 1930s a large munitions factory provided much local revenue. However, passenger numbers inevitably declined in the 1950s and in January 1960 British Railways withdrew its passenger services. Freight trains continued much as before, but stopped using the line between Chorley and Feniscowles in 1966. Two years later the whole branch was decommissioned.

Delph Branch

Passenger service withdrawn	2 May 1955	*Stations closed*	*Date*
Distance	1.5 miles	Delph	2 May 1955
Company	Huddersfield & Manchester Railway &	Measurements Halt	2 May 1955
	Canal Company	Dobcross	2 May 1955
		Moorgate Halt	2 May 1955

A 2-6-2T Class 3P locomotive, No. 40012, and coaches Nos. 15846 and 3484, at Delph Station with the 4.40 p.m. service from Oldham, 19 April 1954.

This short branch opened in 1851, initially using horses to pull carriages along its tracks from Delph to Greenfield. This was inevitably slow and the service quickly acquired the nickname of 'The Delph Donkey'. Steam power was finally introduced in 1856 by which time the adjoining Oldham Mumps to Greenfield line had opened, thus allowing through services to Delph. From 1912 the LNWR, which had absorbed the line, introduced motor-trains and services along the branch greatly improved. This led to a growth in the residential districts around Delph and Oldham and these soon contributed considerable numbers of daily commuters using the line. However, it was these very passengers who turned their backs on the line after the Second World War and took to using their own motor cars to travel to and from work each day. Unable to compete effectively with this trend and facing increasing losses, British Railways had no option but to withdraw all passenger services from the branch during 1955. Freight trains continued to use it intermittently until late 1963.

Garstang – Knott End

Passenger service withdrawn	31 March 1930	*Stations closed*	*Date*
Distance	11.5 miles	Preesall	31 March 1930
Company	Garstang & Knott End Railway	Pilling	31 March 1930
		Nateby *	31 March 1930
Stations closed	*Date*	Garstang Town **	31 March 1930
Knott End	31 March 1930	Garstang & Catterall ***	3 February 1969

Detraining horses at Knott End Station, 27 June 1909.

* Originally known as Winmarleigh until 1 January 1902.
** Originally known as Garstang until 2 June 1924.

** This station remained open for passenger services after 1930 due to its position on the West Coast Main Line.

Preesall Station.

During 1864 a group of prospectors gained parliamentary approval to build a branch line from Garstang & Catterall Station, 9 miles north of Preston on the existing Lancaster & Preston Junction Railway, westwards across a desolate area of reclaimed mossland to the hamlet of Knott End, on the banks of the River Wyre, where there was a local ferry crossing to the growing town of Fleetwood. The low-lying land required little major engineering work, but the newly formed Garstang & Knott End Railway (G&KER) lacked sufficient capital. By 1870 only 7 miles of single track had been laid as far as the village of Pilling. In December of that year the G&KER began operating a limited passenger service using a hired locomotive named 'Hebe' and a couple of old carriages. Two intermediate stops at Garstang and Winmarleigh were opened along the route. In March 1872 'Hebe' had to be taken out of service for a few days for repairs and with the G&KER unable to afford its hire rates the locomotive's owners withdrew their consent for its use. Consequently, the G&KER was forced to struggle on using horses to pull its carriages and by the end of 1872 the entire line had fallen into disuse. Not surprisingly the G&KER filed for bankruptcy and in 1875 an official receiver was appointed to oversee the company's affairs. This enabled goods traffic along the line to restart using an 0-4-0 tank engine. Passenger trains began again in May of that year and during 1876 a second locomotive was brought in. However, revenue from the line was still poor and the receiver had to be reappointed during 1878.

Garstang & Catterall Station, looking towards Preston, 14 July 1957.

Twenty years later a separate company called the Knott End Railway (KER) was created to finally extend the branch from Pilling to its original intended terminus. However, the KER was also plagued by financial difficulties and only the opening of a saltworks at nearby Preesall saved it as it allowed the company to earn valuable trade. It also enabled it to raise enough money to absorb the G&KER in July 1908. Later that very month a full passenger service was introduced all the way to Knott End using an 0-6-0 side tank and a 2-6-0 tank called 'Blackpool'. From 1920 onwards steam-powered railmotor cars were hired from the LNWR. After 1923 the line became the property of the LMS. Passenger services continued much as before using the railmotors, but demand was never great and profits were small. In March 1930 the LMS decided to cut its losses and formally withdrew all passenger trains from the line. Freight services continued but the local industrial decline after 1947 meant that only a single goods train worked the branch each day. Clearly this was uneconomical and in November 1950 British Railways withdrew all services beyond Pilling. Services continued to terminate there until it too was closed in July 1963, while Garstang Town survived in use until August 1965 when what remained of the branch was finally taken out of use.

Great Harwood – Rose Grove

Passenger service withdrawn	3 December 1957	*Stations closed*	*Date*
Distance	9 miles	Great Harwood	30 November 1957
Company	Lancashire & Yorkshire Railway	Padiham	30 November 1957
		Simonstone	30 November 1957

Great Harwood Station, *c*.1912.

In order to connect the mill towns of Great Harwood and Padiham to its growing rail network throughout Lancashire the L&Y built a short branch line from a junction 1½ miles east of Blackburn to the industrialised areas of Padiham and Great Harwood. Due to engineering difficulties the line did not open until 1877 and although goods traffic at first had priority, passenger trains were introduced within a year. The branch also became useful as an avoiding route to bypass the congested railways of Accrington. During the summer months it also served as a through route for holiday trains from east Lancashire and Yorkshire as they headed for Blackpool. The familiarly depressing post-war downturn in rail business blighted the branch during the 1950s and in December 1957 its role as a passenger line ended. Freight trains continued to operate along its length until late 1964, although in ever decreasing numbers.

Lancaster – Glasson Dock

		Stations closed	Date
Passenger service withdrawn	7 July 1930	Condor Green	7 July 1930
Distance	5 miles	Glasson Dock	7 July 1930
Company	London & North Western Railway		

A view taken on the Lancaster – Glasson Dock branch.

Glasson Dock, *c.*1900.

Up to the historic county capital of Lancaster the River Lune was only navigable by small boats and suffered from serious silting. To enable larger ships to serve Lancaster a new port facility was opened at Glasson on the south side of the Lune Estuary during 1787. From 1826 this port was connected to Lancaster by the Lancaster Canal, which enabled small coastal vessels to sail right into the heart of the city. From 1864 the canal was leased to the LNWR but the company sought to speed up services to Glasson by building a rail link from Lancaster Station in 1883. An intermediate halt was established at Condor Green, one mile from where the line terminated at Glasson Dock. Passenger numbers using this branch were never great and the opening of larger harbour amenities at Preston in 1892 significantly reduced the amount of freight passing through Glasson. Somehow the line struggled on into LMS ownership but the Great Depression finally finished it off and the last passenger trains were withdrawn during 1930. Freight, however, continued to ply up and down for a further 34 years before the line was entirely closed during the Beeching era.

Liverpool, Southport & Preston Junction Railway

Passenger service withdrawn	26 September 1938		*Stations closed*	*Date*
Distance	7 miles		Downholland *	26 September 1938
Company	Liverpool, Southport & Preston Junction Railway		Halsall	26 September 1938

Stations closed	*Date*
Shirdley Hill	26 September 1938

* Originally known as Barton until 1924.

Halsall Station, *c.*1905.

This double-tracked line was virtually a branch of the West Lancashire Railway (WLR) and formed a triangular junction with that company's line to Preston and the Southport & Cheshire Lines Extension Railway (S&CLE) at Altcar & Hillhouse. Although nominally independent the Liverpool, Southport & Preston Junction Railway (LS&PJ) was created as a WLR concept so as to provide it with access into Liverpool via the S&CLE. In September 1887 the line was ready as far as Barton and freight services commenced running there from Meols Cop. The following month services were extended to Altcar and a passenger service began in November 1887 to connect with S&CLE trains there heading to or from Liverpool. As the LS&PJ was such a small concern its trains were provided by the WLR and later on by the L&Y. Despite its potential to act as a direct route between Preston and Liverpool, passenger numbers were always low and the line constantly struggled to make any money. The L&Y introduced a steam railmotor service from 1906 and these quickly became known locally as 'Altcar Bobs'. However, passenger numbers still failed to increase substantially and once the line passed into the ownership of the LMS services between Downholland and Altcar were withdrawn in November 1926. Trains to Meols Cop continued to run until September 1938 before they too were taken away. Goods traffic survived until January 1952.

Lowton St Mary's – St Helens

Passenger service withdrawn	3 March 1952
Distance	8.25 miles
Company	St Helens & Wigan Junction Railway

Stations closed	*Date*
Lowton St Mary's *	2 November 1964

Stations closed	*Date*
Golborne North **	3 March 1952
Ashton-in-Makerfield	3 March 1952
Haydock	3 March 1952
St Helens Central ***	3 March 1952

Ashton-in-Makerfield Station.

* This station remained open to passenger services after 1952 due to its position on the Wigan – Glazebrook line.

** Originally known as Golborne until 1 February 1949.
*** Originally known as St Helens until 1 March 1949.

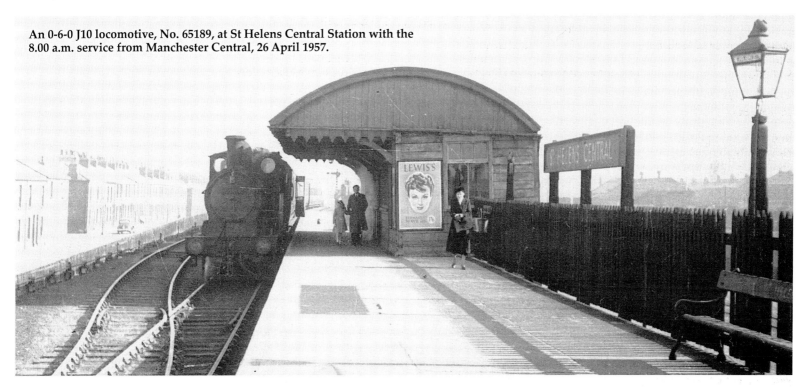

An 0-6-0 J10 locomotive, No. 65189, at St Helens Central Station with the 8.00 a.m. service from Manchester Central, 26 April 1957.

This branch from Lowton St Mary's on the Wigan Junction Railway's (WJR) Glazebrook – Wigan line to the town of St Helens was incorporated in 1885. Although built by the St Helens & Wigan Junction Railway (SH&WJ), running rights for it were granted to the WJR and its backer, the Manchester, Sheffield & Lincolnshire Railway. The construction process was a slow one and while the line was still being built the SH&WJ changed its name in 1889 to become the Liverpool, St Helens & South Lancashire Railway (LSH&SL). Initially, the branch was double-tracked from Lowton St Mary's as far as Ashton-in-Makerfield, from where it was singled into St Helens Central Station. Goods trains began in 1895 and from January 1900 (by which time the whole line was double-tracked) passenger services began with the Great Central Railway (GCR) providing the rolling stock on behalf of the adjoining WJR. Connections to Manchester for trains from St Helens could be made at Lowton St Mary's and a fierce rivalry broke out between the branch and its nearest competitor, the LNWR-sponsored St Helens – Wigan line. In 1906 the GCR took over both the WJR and LSH&SL. In turn the GCR became part of the LNER after the 1923 Groupings. The contest for passengers with the St Helens – Wigan line severely reduced the branch's effectiveness, although large numbers of racegoers frequented it whenever there was a meeting at the Haydock Park course. Special trains were often provided just for the purpose of transporting racing fans to the course. Even after regular passenger services along the branch had ended in 1952, the station at Haydock Park remained active just to serve the nearby racecourse. A private goods siding at Ashton-in-Makerfield also stayed open and in 1967 this was developed to serve as Shell UK Oil's Haydock Terminal. To permit easier access to this facility a new stretch of line was installed from the WCML at Golborne Junction, thus enabling what remained of the Lowton St Mary's branch to be removed.

Middleton Junction – Oldham Werneth

Passenger service withdrawn	2 June 1958	*Stations closed*	*Date*
Distance	2 miles	Middleton Junction *	3 January 1966
Company	Manchester & Leeds Railway		

* Originally known as Oldham Junction until 1842 and then as Middleton until 1852. It remained open to passenger services after 1958 due to its position on the line from Manchester to Rochdale via Newton Heath.

The planned direction of the Manchester & Leeds Railway (M&L) passed close by the town of Oldham and in 1839 the company won the right to build a branch into the town from Middleton Junction, close to its station at Mills Hill. Designed by George Stephenson, the branch opened in 1842 and terminated at a new station called Oldham Werneth on the western side of the town. This location was 525 feet above sea level and to reach it a climb of 1 in 27 was involved which meant that trains had to be assisted by a series of ropes and pulleys. From November 1847 the branch was linked via tunnels to the nearby station at Oldham Mumps and by 1854 newer steam locomotive designs meant that the use of ropes and pulleys could come to an end. Due to the line's steep gradients it was used to test the benefits of continuous train braking during 1859 and these trials proved generally successful. From May 1880 a new line into Oldham Werneth was opened from Thorpes Bridge Junction, but services along the original route continued much as before. Passenger numbers continued to hold up and the line eventually became the property of the L&Y and later the LMS. Officially passenger services ended in June 1958, but the branch remained open for goods traffic and the occasional diverted passenger train until May 1960. The Diesel Multiple Units (DMUs) that often constituted these diverted services were sometimes unable to make it up the line's severe climb. An enthusiasts' charter made the last recorded passenger trip along the branch in September 1960 and the last known goods train worked the line in January 1963.

Middleton Junction Station, 20 April 1951.

Morecambe – Hest Bank

Passenger service withdrawn	15 September 1958	*Stations closed*	*Date*
Distance	2.5 miles	Morecambe Poulton Lane *	9 May 1886
Company	London & North Western Railway	Morecambe Euston Road **	15 September 1958
		Hest Bank ***	3 February 1969
		Bolton-le-Sands ***	3 February 1969

Morecambe Euston Road Station.

* Replaced by Morecambe in 1886 (this was renamed Morecambe Euston Road in 1924).
** Originally known as Morecambe until 2 June 1924.

*** These stations remained open to passenger services due to their positions on the West Coast Main Line. Bolton-le-Sands was originally known as Bolton until 1861.

Bare Lane Station. Still in service, this station lies between Morecambe and the location of Hest Bank Station. Originally known as Poulton-le-Sands, it opened on 12 June 1848 and was renamed on 31 October 1864.

The LNWR was slow to take an interest in providing a rail service into Morecambe and it wasn't until 1864 that the company decided to act. It built a branch line from Hest Bank (on the former Lancaster & Carlisle Railway's main line route) to a new station in Morecambe named Poulton Lane. Two years later this was replaced by a new facility at Euston Road. A connection with the neighbouring North Western Railway (absorbed into the MR in 1871) was also included. The LNWR's line was always overshadowed by its MR competitor, although from the late 1920s (when the LMS ran both routes) it did enjoy a spell as a through-link for boat trains travelling on to Heysham. However, during the 1950s British Railways transferred most local trains to Morecambe Promenade and this led to the closure of the station at Euston Road during September 1958. However, the branch remained unofficially in use until September 1963 for summer Saturday holiday traffic heading into Morecambe. Hest Bank, thanks to its spot on the WCML, survived a little longer than the branch it once served and did not close for a further six years.

Morecambe – Heysham

Passenger service withdrawn	8 October 1975	*Stations closed*	*Date*
Distance	4 miles	Heysham Harbour	4 May 1970
Company	Midland Railway	Middleton Road Bridge Halt	31 June 1905

The MR obtained its right to construct a short line from Morecambe to nearby Heysham during 1892. This was fortuitous as the harbour facilities at Morecambe were no longer adequate for continued steamer trips to Ireland whereas a developed Heysham could, despite its proximity to the existing port of Fleetwood. Local passenger trains between Morecambe's existing Northumberland Street Station and Heysham Harbour commenced in 1904 using steam railmotors (otherwise known as 'motor cars') and an intermediate halt was set up at Middleton Road. The railmotors only lasted until 1905 when they were transferred elsewhere and Middleton Road was closed due to a lack of local demand. By this time sailings between Heysham and Belfast had begun, while crossings to Dublin and Londonderry had been transferred down from Morecambe. Sailings to the Isle of Man also started up soon after. In 1907 the new station at Morecambe Promenade opened and a connecting spur linked that facility to the rival LNWR's Euston Road station in the town. When the line down to Heysham was electrified in 1908, EMUs took over most passenger shuttles between the two neighbouring towns. After 1923 the branch became the responsibility of the LMS who introduced through boat trains from London Euston and Manchester to Heysham, rather than using Fleetwood as before. Sailings to Belfast continued to prosper throughout the 1920s and '30s, thus keeping the line busy. Private sidings were also added during the Second World War to cater for nearby oil and chemical factories plus an Air Ministry establishment that was full of military personnel. The pioneering EMUs were finally taken out of service in 1966 and during May 1970 a completely rebuilt Heysham Harbour Station opened next to the site of the original one. Between 1970 and '72 the line saw a growth in services as most Holyhead trains were diverted along it due to the Britannia Bridge fire which closed all rail access to Anglesey. These trains, mostly parcel services, connected at Heysham with boats bound for Dun Laoghaire in Ireland. This boom was all too brief for once services to Holyhead were restored this Welsh port quickly became the focus for crossings of the Irish Sea. Sailings from Heysham to Belfast declined sharply and ended totally during 1975. In the autumn of that same year the last passenger trains ran between Morecambe and Heysham before the service was withdrawn. In 1978 ferry crossings to the Isle of Man restarted but the former rail link to Heysham was not revived.

Heysham Harbour Station, 13 May 1966.

Oldham – Guide Bridge

Passenger service withdrawn	4 May 1959	*Stations closed*	*Date*
Distance	6.25 miles	Oldham Clegg Street	4 May 1959
Company	Oldham, Ashton & Guide Bridge Railway	Park Bridge	4 May 1959
		Ashton Oldham Road	4 May 1959
		Ashton Moss	1 June 1862

Oldham Clegg Street Station, looking towards Greenfield, 12 April 1957.

Park Bridge Station.

The Oldham, Ashton & Guide Bridge Railway (OA&GB) was incorporated in 1857 with the backing of the LNWR and the Manchester, Sheffield & Lincolnshire Railway (MS&L) to build a railway from Oldham via Ashton-under-Lyne to Guide Bridge. This new line would provide a link from the LNWR at Oldham Mumps to the L&Y at Ashton and on down to Guide Bridge. This second stretch was actually the first to be completed during 1860, but the Oldham – Ashton portion of the line was delayed by the need to build a viaduct over the Medlock at Park Bridge, plus two short tunnels and a high embankment. As a result it was not completed until late 1861. Once the branch was fully finished, passenger services began at once with the MS&L running trains from Manchester to Ashton and then on to Oldham where the line was served by a new station at Clegg Street. Localised services also operated between Oldham and Guide Bridge and to maximise local interest the OA&GB provided a complimentary omnibus link to Rochdale until 1863 when the L&Y thwarted that scheme by opening its own direct rail link between the two towns. The MS&L's dominance over train services using the branch lasted until 1872. The following year the company was forced to run an equal share of services alongside the LNWR. The creation of a local tram network in the early 1900s hit the OA&GB hard. Despite declining passenger numbers the line survived until after the Second World War when British Railways cut back operations along it even further. Once the last passenger train had run in 1959, a new parcels-handling depot was opened up at Oldham Clegg Street. This kept the line relatively busy until May 1967 when it was finally closed permanently.

Ormskirk – Rainford – St Helens

Passenger service withdrawn   18 June 1951 (St Helens – Rainford Junction);
5 November 1956 (Rainford Junction – Ormskirk)
Distance   11.5 miles in total
Companies   St Helens Railway (St Helens – Rainford Junction);
East Lancashire Railway (Rainford Junction – Ormskirk)

Stations closed	*Date*
Skelmersdale *	5 November 1956
Gerard's Bridge	1 August 1905

* Originally named Blaguegate until 1874.

Skelmersdale Station.

In 1848 the L&Y opened its Liverpool – Bury line just north of the village of Rainford. Nearby, local coal mines were beginning to spring up around the village of Skelmersdale and their owners soon began pressing for a local rail link. Early proposals all failed to make the grade and it was not until 1853 that the East Lancashire Railway (ELR) gained approval to build a line from Ormskirk to Skelmersdale and on to Rainford. This upset the St Helens Railway & Canal Company which, in 1853, had also gained permission to build its own line from St Helens to Rainford. Despite the St Helens Railway's objections, both planned lines went ahead and opened simultaneously in 1858 to provide a through route from Ormskirk to St Helens with spurs linking on to the L&Y through Rainford Junction. The ELR was the first to begin passenger operations when it began running trains from Ormskirk to Rainford Junction. From there passengers were eventually able to change onto trains provided by the St Helens Railway to continue their journeys. In 1859 the ELR was absorbed by the L&Y and five years after this the LNWR took over the St Helens Railway and granted the L&Y full running rights over its metals between Rainford Junction and St Helens. In 1906 the L&Y introduced a railmotor service along the line between Ormskirk and Rainford Junction and this was later extended all the way to St Helens. The stretch of line from Rainford Junction down to St Helens served few sizeable population centres, but somehow managed to survive into British Railways ownership whereupon it was promptly closed down during 1951. Passenger services between Ormskirk and Rainford Junction, however, were slightly more popular and these managed to continue until November 1956. Five years after the last passenger train ran along the branch the village of Skelmersdale was earmarked to become a New Town and ironically its residential population later soared. The line was still important for goods traffic and a key source of this was the Pilkington Glass Company's sand-washing plant at Old Mill Lane and its glass factory near Gerard's Bridge in St Helens. However, this one major customer was insufficient to prevent freight services being withdrawn between Rainford Junction and Skelmersdale during 1961. Staged withdrawals then continued as more and more freight switched to road haulage and by July 1964 all services along the line had ended.

Pennington – Platt Bridge

Passenger service withdrawn	21 September 1963	*Stations closed*	*Date*
Distance	3.5 miles	Plank Lane	22 February 1915
Company	London & North Western Railway	Platt Bridge	1 May 1961

In an effort to capture as much of the south Lancashire coal traffic as it could, the LNWR opened a short double-tracked branch from Pennington on the Bolton – Kenyon Junction line to Platt Bridge on the nearby Tydesley – Wigan line. This enabled the collieries at Plank Lane and Bickershaw to be rail served. Originally opened for freight services in March 1885, the branch began running passenger trains from late 1903 after an avoiding section was built around Pennington which allowed passenger services from Leigh to reach Platt Bridge and then Wigan or Manchester. By 1910 the LNWR was running three passenger trains per day along the branch in each direction. The station at Plank Lane closed during the First World War but passenger operations continued using the line in diminishing numbers until 1939. Workers trains serving Bickershaw Colliery continued to run until September 1963. Freight remained the line's lifeblood and after the end of passenger services a single-track was kept *in situ* between Bickershaw and Wigan solely to handle bulk coal trains to and from the local mine.

Preston – Longridge

Longridge Station.

Passenger service withdrawn	2 June 1930
Distance	6.5 miles
Company	Preston & Longridge Railway

Stations closed	*Date*
Longridge	2 June 1930
Preston Maudland Bridge	1 June 1885
Deepdale *	2 June 1930
Ribbleton **	2 June 1930
Grimsargh	2 June 1930

* Originally called Deepdale Bridge until 1867.
** Originally called Gamull Lane until 1856 and then renamed Fulwood until 1900.

Ribbleton Station.

Built to carry stone from the quarry at Longridge Fell to Preston and on to Liverpool, this line was opened in March 1839 by the Preston & Longridge Railway Company (P&L). Actual train services, however, did not commence until the following year and although chiefly intended as a goods line there was a passenger train every Wednesday and Saturday. During 1846 the P&L became involved in a bold expansion scheme to link Fleetwood with the Leeds & Bradford Railway via Clitheroe and Elslack. This plan came to nought bar a connection between the P&L and its close ally, the Preston & Wyre. Two years later the P&L switched from using horses to pull carriages along its tracks to steam locomotives. By 1856 the company had been absorbed into the Fleetwood, Preston & West Riding Junction Railway and had opened a new terminus in Preston at Deepdale.

Grimsargh Station.

The line to Longridge eventually passed into the joint ownership of the LNWR and L&Y during 1867 and the following year a private extension was opened from Grimsargh to the mental hospital at Whittingham. As well as carrying hospital staff and patients, this line also supplied local coal and stores. The growing competition from bus firms was the killer blow to the branch's existence and in June 1930 all passenger services were formally withdrawn. Goods traffic continued, especially to the Courtaulds factory near Grimsargh, as did services to Whittingham Hospital (which ran until June 1957). Overall, however, the line continued to wither away, especially after stone movements from Longridge Fell ended in the 1950s. On 6 November 1967 the final goods train ran to Longridge and by July of the following year much of the line's trackwork had already been lifted. By early 1980 only a very small stretch remained *in situ* around Deepdale, serving as a siding to Preston Power Station until the last trains had run to Courtaulds that summer.

Preston Road – Fleetwood

Passenger service withdrawn	1 June 1970	*Stations closed*	*Date*
Distance	19.75 miles	Thornton-Cleveleys ***	1 June 1970
Company	Preston & Wyre Railway & Harbour Company	Singleton	2 May 1932
		Ramper	2 April 1843
Stations closed	*Date*	Weeton	2 April 1843
Fleetwood *	18 April 1966	Lea Road	2 May 1938
Fleetwood **	1 June 1970		

Fleetwood Station (the one which closed in 1966), c.1908.

* This replaced a station of the same name which was open between 1840 and 1883.
** Originally named Wyre Dock until 18 April 1966.

*** Originally named Cleveleys until 1905, then Thornton-for-Cleveleys until February 1953.

Thanks to the efforts of one Sir Peter Hesketh Fleetwood, the local MP, the Preston & Wyre Railway (P&W) was incorporated in 1835. The following year Sir Peter founded an industrial harbour town beside the River Wyre estuary near Burn Naze and called it Wyreton. At the same time he also planned to build a seaside resort nearby which was named Fleetwood in his honour. The P&W was tasked with building a railway to serve these towns from Preston and so the three projects became interlinked. In July 1840 the first passenger trains reached Fleetwood from Preston and to attract customers the P&W bought a steamer for sailings from Fleetwood to Bardsea, Belfast and the Isle of Man. This resulted in over 108,000 passengers using the line within its first year of opening. Between 1846 and '47 the branch was doubled-tracked as far as Burn Naze and an alternative route around the Wyre Estuary was added. While this was under construction the P&W was jointly taken over by the LNWR and L&Y during 1849 and two years later the alternative route was opened to trains. Soon after this, structural faults with the original line, particularly along its stone embankment across the Wyre, led to the alternative route being double-tracked from 1875 so that it could become the principal way into Fleetwood. After the 1923 Groupings the line passed into the hands of the LMS. Passenger numbers using the line dipped after 1928 when the steamer service to Belfast switched to Heysham, but the most noticeable decline occurred after the Second World War when much of the line's business was lost to other routes as shipping firms relocated to rival ports. By the 1960s Fleetwood's dock facilities were in serious need of an upgrade, but the costs involved did not justify the amount of shipping still using the port. As a result Fleetwood Station closed in 1966 along with sections of the branch line leading up to it. Consequently, Wyre Dock Station was renamed Fleetwood but all passenger services to and from it ceased in 1970. A section of the line however remained in use for goods traffic only to serve the chemical works at Burn Naze.

Rochdale – Bacup

Passenger service withdrawn	16 June 1947		
Distance	5 miles		
Company	Lancashire & Yorkshire Railway		

Stations closed	*Date*
Britannia	2 April 1917
Facit	16 June 1947

Stations closed	*Date*
Whitworth	16 June 1947
Bacup *	5 December 1966

* This station remained open to passenger services after 1947 because it was the terminus for two routes from Rochdale and Bury (via Rawtenstall). When the Rochdale route closed in 1947, the Bury line remained open as part of the East Lancashire Railway.

An 0-6-0 3F locomotive, No. 52443, at Bacup Station with the 3.54 p.m. service to Bury, 23 April 1954.

This branch was a typical example of a railway company building a line in the knowledge that while it would never make a profit it would keep a competitor out of the area. In this case the L&Y wished to keep the Manchester, Sheffield & Lincolnshire Railway out of the Rochdale district. Construction work on the line was dogged by difficulties. A hugely expensive viaduct had to be built at Rochdale, while around Facit a climb of 1 in 50 had to be overcome. Closer to Bacup the line had to become single-tracked for much of its length due to the surrounding terrain, which was steep as well as undulating, and this caused frequent landslides during the building phase. Despite these engineering nightmares, the line between Rochdale and Facit was ready by October 1870. Passenger trains began a month later and a double-tracked extension into Bacup, where the line terminated at the East Lancashire Railway's existing station in the town, was finished during 1881. This final stretch of track climbed gradients as great as 1 in 34 to a height of 965 feet above sea level. As anticipated the volume of traffic and passengers using the line was poor from the start, yet amazingly services continued until June 1947. Even when passenger trains had ceased using the branch, freight continued to ply its metals (though no further than Facit after 1963) until August 1967 when the final goods train worked the remaining section between Rochdale and Whitworth.

Roe Green Junction – Bolton

Passenger service withdrawn	29 March 1954	*Stations closed*	*Date*
Distance	12 miles	Walkden Low Level *	29 March 1954
Company	London & North Western Railway	Little Hulton	29 March 1954
		Plodder Lane	29 March 1954

* Originally known as Walkden until 2 June 1924.

Walkden Low Level Station.

WALKDEN LOW LEVEL

In mid-1870 the LNWR opened this branch from Roe Green Junction, near Worsley on the Eccles Junction – Springs branch, to the pits at Little Hulton. Four years later it was extended to Great Moor Street Station in Bolton for the transfer of freight services. From 1875 a passenger service began and soon services were running via the branch from Bolton into Manchester Victoria. The line also enabled the LNWR to lay on through-carriages from Bolton to London Euston using the South Junction link in Manchester and the nearby London Road Station. Plodder Lane was also developed as a locomotive shed and gained an allocation of 0-6-2 tanks for branch passenger operations and larger 0-8-0s for heavy coal trains. Smaller goods work was usually handled by the shed's consignment of Webb 0-6-0s. After 1923 the LMS took over the line and began introducing ex-MR Class 4F 0-6-0s and former L&Y 2-4-2 tanks. Electric trams and, later on, bus companies quickly proved a major threat to the line's survival and this rivalry only intensified during the 1950s despite the introduction of Ivatt or Standard Class 2 2-6-2 tank locomotives by British Railways in a bid to improve efficiency. Eventually, the branch lost its passenger service in 1954 due to lack of demand. The stretch of line between Bolton and the collieries at Little Hulton continued to see some use until May 1964, three years after the rest of the branch had been taken out of service. Today, the former locomotive shed at Plodder Lane is a residential area.

Southport – Preston

Passenger service withdrawn	7 September 1964		*Stations closed*	*Date*
Distance	9.5 miles		Hesketh Bank	7 September 1964
Company	West Lancashire Railway		Hoole	7 September 1964
			Longton Bridge	7 September 1964
			New Longton & Hutton *	7 September 1964
Stations closed	*Date*		Penwortham Cop Lane *	7 September 1964
Southport Central	1 May 1901		Preston Fishergate Hill	1902
Hesketh Park	7 September 1964			
Churchtown	7 September 1964			
Crossens	7 September 1964		* Originally named Howick until 1897, then Hutton & Howick until 1934.	
Banks	7 September 1964		* Originally known as Cop Lane Halt until 1940.	
Hundred End	30 April 1962			

Hesketh Bank Station, *c.1915.*

Hutton & Howick Station (later renamed New Longton & Hutton).

The West Lancashire Railway (WLR) was authorised in 1871 to build a new railway from the growing coastal resort of Southport to Preston through an area of countryside that was sparsely populated and dominated by agriculture. In Preston the line was to terminate at a brand new station named Fishergate Hill. The WLR opened in February 1878 as far as Hesketh Bank, but it was not until September 1882 that the line finally opened along its entire length even though Preston's Fishergate Hill was still not ready nor was the other terminus at Southport Central. Not surprisingly local passenger numbers were less than expected due to the rural nature of the area through which much of the line had been built. In 1886 the WLR entered official receivership and was eventually bought by the L&Y in 1897. As a result of this move, most trains using the line then began or ended their journeys from the L&Y's Chapel Street Station in Southport and eventually Southport Central became little more than a goods depot. The station at Fishergate Hill in Preston also closed during 1900 as a new connection at Whitehouse North Junction gave trains approaching from Southport access to the L&Y's joint station in the town. However, it was reactivated two years after closure to cater for visitors flocking into Preston for the Guild Festival and thereafter it remained in use as a goods facility. Part of the branch between Southport and Crossens was electrified when the L&Y pioneered the use of EMUs on its Liverpool – Southport services. This led to a regular suburban EMU train operating along this section of the branch and it soon proved extremely popular. During the 1950s, while other lines were trying to cut costs and improve efficiency by switching over from steam to DMUs, the old WLR line saw increasing use of powerful Class 5 4-6-0 locomotives hauling lightly loaded trains of just two or three carriages! The line's overall poor economy and low passenger numbers (despite the well-used electrified stretch from Southport to Crossens) soon caught Dr Beeching's eye. In September 1964 the last passenger trains were operated, although goods traffic – which had never been a prominent feature of the WLR – carried on until January 1965.

Stubbins – Accrington Branch

Passenger service withdrawn	5 December 1966	*Stations closed*	*Date*
Distance	7.25 miles	Helmshore	5 December 1966
Company	East Lancashire Railway	Haslingden	7 November 1960
		Baxenden	10 September 1951
Stations	*Date closed*		
Stubbins *	5 June 1972	* After 1966 this station remained open to passengers using Bury – Bacup services.	

Haslingden Station, 23 April 1954.

Originally incorporated as the Blackburn, Burnley, Accrington & Colne Extension Railway in 1845, this line was intended to provide a link from the town of Stubbins on the East Lancashire Railway northwards to the larger town of Accrington. However, before work on the line could begin the East Lancashire Railway (ELR) absorbed it and took over responsibility for its construction as it intended turning Accrington into a key junction for its planned routes west towards Blackburn and east for Colne. From Stubbins the branch climbed for 5 miles at a rate of 1 in 78 through the villages of Helmshore and Haslingden to reach a summit at Baxenden, 771 feet above sea level. From there the line dropped sharply (often by as much as 1 in 38) for 2¼ miles into Accrington. This stretch later became known as the Baxenden Bank. Upon opening in August 1848, the branch became useful as a through route for Manchester–Colne services (once the ELR's line to the latter had opened in 1849). In fact this became the branch's key purpose with up to fourteen weekday trains between Manchester and Colne traversing its length by 1882. Local passenger numbers were never particularly high and in 1951 Baxenden Station closed due to a lack of demand. The branch however remained popular for Manchester–Colne trains until 1964 when these services were rationalised on the grounds of cost and economy. Thereafter, it became impossible to travel direct from Manchester to Colne via the Stubbins line. The Beeching Report signalled the end for the line and in 1966 it was finally closed to all passenger and goods traffic. The trackbed remained *in situ* until 1970/71 when it was finally lifted.

Wennington – Lancaster – Morecambe

Passenger service withdrawn	3 January 1966	*Stations closed*	*Date*
Distance	13.5 miles	Claughton	1 August 1853
Company	North Western Railway	Halton	3 January 1966
		Caton	1 May 1961
Stations closed	*Date*	Hornby	16 September 1957
Lancaster Green Ayre *	3 January 1966	Scale Hall	3 January 1966
Wray	1 June 1850		

Line repairs at Lancaster Green Ayre Station.

* Originally named Lancaster until 1850, then Lancaster Green Area until 1870.

Caton Station, c.1916.

In 1846 the North Western Railway (NWR) gained permission to begin work on a branch line (originally single-tracked but subsequently doubled) linking the coastal resort of Morecambe with Lancaster and then on to Wennington in the Lune Valley. From Wennington a link to the Midland's main line between Ingleton and Skipton (then under construction) was provided. As the NWR was short of money it concentrated its efforts on completing the Lancaster – Morecambe stretch and this opened in June 1848. In Lancaster a new station was built at Green Area (later renamed Green Ayre) while over at Morecambe the original terminus was known as Poulton (becoming simply Morecambe after 1850). The line from Lancaster to Wennington opened in November 1849 and the following month a connection from the NWR's station at Green Area was added to meet the rival Lancaster & Carlisle Railway's stop at Lancaster Castle. From 1852, the NWR entered into an agreement with the MR for the latter to work services along the line, which was enjoying something of a boom thanks to steamer sailings from Morecambe to Ireland. In January 1871 the MR absorbed the NWR completely and began work on doubling the branch in stages, a process that was completed by 1889. By the late nineteenth century Morecambe had outlived its usefulness as a port and so concentrated on its role as a holiday centre, while nearby Heysham was specifically developed with the help of the MR to handle steamer traffic. To acknowledge Morecambe's revised priorities, a new station was opened in the town at the Promenade during 1907 and from here a subsidiary line ran down the coast to Heysham.

During 1908 part of the line between Lancaster and Morecambe was electrified using high-voltage, single-phase AC power rated at 6,600 volts, 25 Hz. The stretch down to Heysham was also wired under this scheme and the MR introduced Derby-built electric motor coaches and trailers to operate passenger services. These pioneering Electric Multiple Units (EMUs) were to remain in use for over forty years. Between Lancaster and Wennington the branch remained steam hauled and provided passengers with a pleasing run through the picturesque Lune Valley. Steam power also returned to the Lancaster – Morecambe section during 1951 when British Railways sought to convert the overhead electrical supply to a 6,600-volt, 50 Hz arrangement. When this work was completed the following year, rebuilt ex-LNWR rolling stock (already nearly four decades old) was introduced to work the line. However, between October 1955 and March 1956 electric services were once again suspended while modifications could be implemented to the power supply system as British Railways wanted to use the line as an experimental facility for testing high-voltage AC arrangements which were later to be used on the electrification of the WCML. By this time passenger numbers had already begun falling due to the widespread increase in car ownership and the advent of local bus services, and although Scale Hall was opened in 1957 in a bid to drum up passenger numbers, in recognition of this decline the intermediate stations along the branch began to close. Then, in January 1966, all passenger services were withdrawn. Green Ayre Station became a goods depot and freight traffic continued to use the branch until June 1967.

Wigan – Glazebrook

Passenger service withdrawn	2 November 1964	*Stations closed*	*Date*
Distance	11.75 miles	Hindley South *	2 November 1964
Company	Wigan Junction Railways Company	Bickershaw & Abram	2 November 1964
		West Leigh & Bedford **	2 November 1964
Stations closed	*Date*	Lowton St Mary's	2 November 1964
Wigan Central	2 November 1964	Culcheth	2 November 1964
Lower Ince	2 November 1964	Glazebrook ***	22 March 1968

Wigan Central Station.

* Originally named Strangeways & Hindley until 1892, then Hindley & Platt Bridge until 1952.
** Originally known as Plank Lane For West Leigh until 1894.

*** This station remained open to passenger services after 1964 due to its position on the CLC's Liverpool – Manchester line.

Bickershaw & Abram Station, looking towards Wigan, 23 August 1952.

The rich coal seams of south Lancashire inevitably attracted the interest of railway developers and in 1873 the Wigan Junction Railways Company (WJR) was formed to build a line from Wigan through the local coalfields to join up with the Cheshire Lines Committee's (CLC) railway at Glazebrook. The scheme was backed by the MR and the Manchester, Sheffield & Lincolnshire Railway (MS&L), although the Midland later withdrew its support in 1877. During October 1879 the line, double-tracked, opened from Glazebrook as far as Strangeways Hall Colliery at Amberswood near Hindley. Coal and other goods trains began running immediately with the MS&L providing the necessary motive power. In April 1884 the line was finally extended to Wigan where a temporary station was opened at Darlington Street to enable passenger services to commence along the branch. From this station a ¼-mile link was added during 1892 to a brand new terminus named Wigan Central. Thereafter, the original Wigan stop became a goods depot. Thanks to its connection with the CLC, the branch was useful for expresses departing Manchester Central that needed to reach Wigan. This could be achieved in about 45 minutes, although services using the rival LNWR's lines could cover a similar distance in 33 to 37 minutes. Once the L&Y's new line via Walkden had been opened a non-stop Wigan to Manchester service could cover the distance in just 24 minutes. It was this time factor that led to the Glazebrook – Wigan line quickly becoming something of a backwater once it became the property of the Great Central Railway in 1906. From 1923 the line formed part of the LNER's network. The Beeching axe fell on the branch during the 1960s as passenger trains between Wigan Central and Glazebrook were withdrawn. Local freight and coal traffic kept the line open until November 1967.

Wigan – Tyldesley – Eccles – Manchester

Passenger service withdrawn	5 May 1969		*Stations closed*	*Date*
Distance	12 miles		Hindley Green	1 May 1961
Company	London & North Western Railway		Pennington **	29 March 1954
			Leigh ***	5 May 1969
Stations closed	*Date*		Monton Green	5 May 1969
Worsley	5 May 1969			
Ellenbrook	2 January 1961		* Originally called Chowbent until April 1901.	
Tyldesley	5 May 1969		** Originally named Bradshaw Leach until 1877.	
Howe Bridge *	20 July 1959		*** Originally named Bedford Leigh until 1876, then Leigh & Bedford until 1914.	

Worsley Station.

This line was opened as a direct route from Eccles, on the Liverpool & Manchester Railway, to Springs Branch, Wigan, by the LNWR in a bid to exploit the local coal and textile revenues around south Lancashire. A 3-mile spur from Tyldesley via Leigh was included to provide a connection with the Bolton – Kenyon Junction line near Pennington. At Wigan (where trains worked to and from the North Union's station, Wigan North Western) the line crossed the Bolton & Leigh Railway so a link was built there to enable services between Manchester and Bolton to operate through Tyldesley. In 1882 a new line was opened from Manchester to Preston avoiding Wigan and so many trains were re-routed to this new link, causing a downturn in the branch's traffic flows. Seven years later the LNWR took over the North Union Railway and set to work enlarging Wigan North Western in the hope that it would become a centre for local passenger operations. However, after the Second World War the nationalised British Railways was less interested in the line's survival due to the decline of local industries around Wigan. In fact, as early as 1942 passenger trains had stopped running between Tyldesley and Bolton and so the writing was clearly on the wall. The end came in November 1964 when all passenger services between Wigan and Tyldesley were withdrawn, although a few holiday workings continued to use the branch until late 1968. Through freight trains ceased in early 1969 and midway through that year services between Liverpool and Manchester stopped using the branch and were routed elsewhere. This led to the closure of the remaining stations, as well as bringing the curtain down on the line's existence once and for all. Much of its path was later used to build a network of local motorways.